Copyright © 2024 by Efua Akoma, PhD

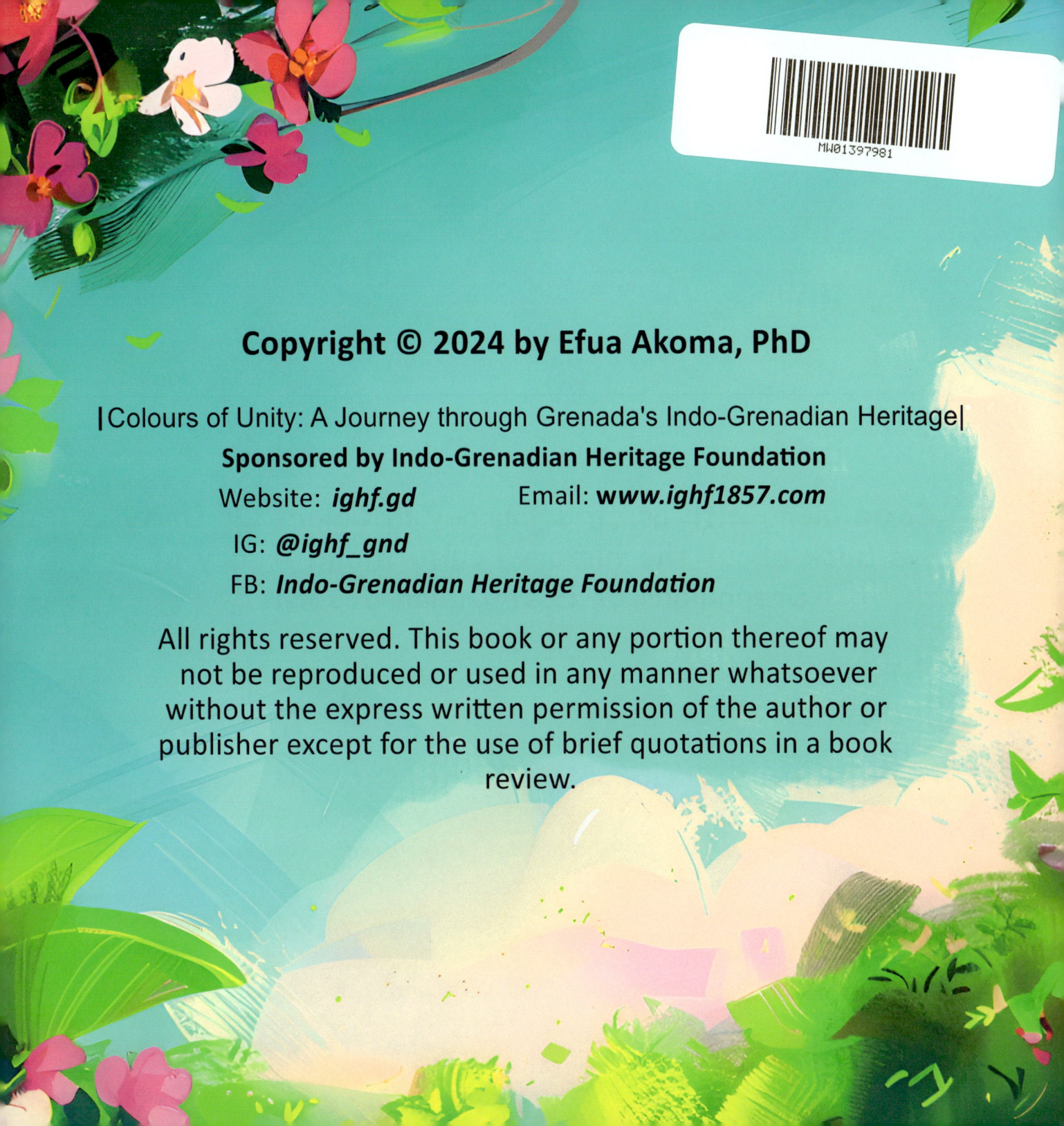

|Colours of Unity: A Journey through Grenada's Indo-Grenadian Heritage|

Sponsored by Indo-Grenadian Heritage Foundation

Website: *ighf.gd*   Email: *www.ighf1857.com*

IG: *@ighf_gnd*

FB: *Indo-Grenadian Heritage Foundation*

All rights reserved. This book or any portion thereof may not be reproduced or used in any manner whatsoever without the express written permission of the author or publisher except for the use of brief quotations in a book review.

Come along with us on a journey in Colors Of Unity, a book about the history, culture and legacy of Grenadians of East Indian descent.

Once upon a time, on the beautiful island of Grenada, a special story is being told about strong people, their unique culture, the community they built and their lasting influences on the nation. Come along with us on a journey through history's pages as we dive into the amazing tale of Grenadians of Indian descent, who we call Indo-Grenadians. This enchanting story is for everyone, young and old, inviting you to discover the vibrant heritage and important contributions of the East Indian community in Grenada. We'll go on an exciting adventure to uncover the lasting spirit and cultural treasures of the Indo-Grenadian people. Get ready for a fantastic voyage into an extraordinary piece of Grenada's cultural identity!

In the year 1857, in a faraway land called India, a group of brave and hopeful individuals embarked on a journey. They chose to travel across the vast, shimmering ocean to a beautiful island called Grenada. The journey was not like the adventures you read in fairy tales. It was a real-life story of strength, resilience, and a quest for a new beginning.

Picture a grand ship with billowing sails, ready to set sail from the shores of India. The people, with excitement and a touch of nervousness, boarded the ship, leaving behind the familiar sights and sounds of their homeland. The ship set course for Grenada, sailing across the deep blue sea, guided by the stars and the promise of a brighter future.

The journey was long and took many weeks. The individuals spent their days on the ship, looking out at the endless expanse of water. Imagine them sharing stories and singing songs to keep their spirits high. They marveled at the vastness of the ocean. Sometimes it seemed like they would never see land again.

The ship faced mighty waves and gentle breezes, all while carrying the dreams and hopes of those aboard. The journey wasn't always easy. There were storms that rocked the ship and moments when the people missed their homes, family and friends. Yet, they held onto the belief that their destination, Grenada, would be a place of opportunity and new beginnings.

Finally, after what felt like the longest adventure ever, the ship approached the shores of Grenada. Those aboard, filled with anticipation, caught their first glimpse of the lush, green landscape and the beauty of this island. The big ship they traveled on was called the Maidstone. It docked on the Carenage in St. Georges, May 1st of 1857, after 89 days of travel on the sea.

Many of those aboard were sick and needed medical attention after being at sea for so long. They got help when they arrived and the following day, they were placed on smaller boats and traveled up to the north of the island.

The individuals disembarked from the smaller ships, carrying with them the strength of their ancestors, and the dreams of a brighter future. They also brought with them their vibrant culture and religious beliefs as well as foods and plants from India. The area in the north they were brought to is called Irwin's Bay in the parish of St. Patrick.

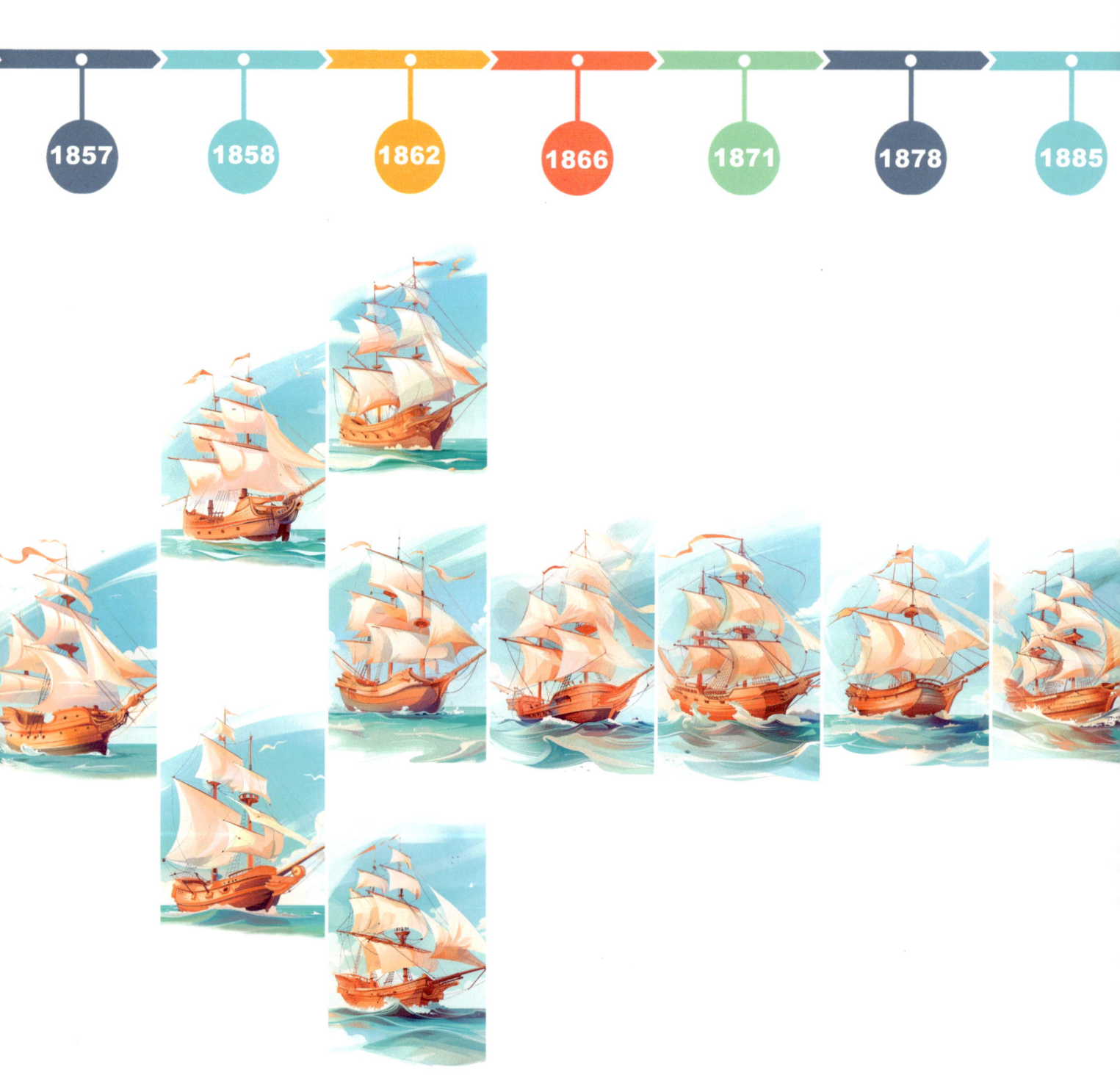

Over the next 28 years, 3,205 East Indians came to Grenada on a total of 10 ships. All of these Indians must have experienced a whirlwind of emotions as they stepped onto the shores of this new and unfamiliar land. Imagine if you had to leave behind the familiar sights, sounds, scents and the people of Grenada. Would that be difficult?

Well, they left behind many things like vibrant markets, the colorful festivals, and the warmth of extended family and friends they held dear. After such a long journey at sea, they found themselves in a place that was, at first, completely different.

The initial feelings of the Indian immigrants may have been a mix of excitement, curiosity, and perhaps a bit of anxiety. They were embarking on a journey into the unknown, driven by hopes for a better life and opportunities that awaited them in Grenada. As they set foot on the island, they were met with a landscape of lush greenery, new faces, and a climate quite different from what they were accustomed to.

Adjusting to this strange land would not have been easy. The Indian immigrants had to learn new customs, adapt to a different climate, and understand the local way of life. They likely faced challenges in communication, as languages may have differed, and they had to navigate a society with its own unique traditions.

However, the strength and resilience of these individuals would have played a crucial role in their adjustment. Over time, they forged connections with one another, forming communities like Fountain, Cuma, Diego Piece, Red Mud and Samaritan. The support and camaraderie within these communities helped ease the transition. As they established roots, learned about the local culture, and contributed to the development of Grenada, the Indians became an integral part of the island's rich tapestry.

The process of adjustment and adaptation may have involved the exchange of cultural practices, the sharing of stories, and the creation of a new, blended identity. While there were undoubtedly moments of challenge and longing for their homeland, the Indo-Grenadians gradually became woven into the fabric of Grenadian society, leaving a lasting impact on the island's history and culture. Their ability to adapt, build communities, and contribute to their new home showcases the resilience of the human spirit in the face of change and the promise of a brighter future.

We know some East Indians came to find a better life but why did Grenada need them? Long ago, after the enslavement of Africans ended in Grenada, the nation was dealing with a labor shortage. With the abolition of slavery there arose a challenge that needed brave hearts to overcome. The sugar plantations faced a shortage of workers, as many recently freed Africans chose to leave the plantations and start a new life elsewhere on the island. This was a new chapter unfolding in the island's history. This is why East Indians under an indentureship scheme were brought to the island, beginning a new chapter.

This Indenture

This crucial moment in history led to the establishment of what became known as the "indentureship scheme." In the face of the labor shortage on the sugar plantations, a solution was sought that involved sourcing labor from distant lands. The scheme unfolded as a means to address this pressing need for workers, and it marked a transformative period for both Grenada and the brave individuals who embarked on this journey.

The indentureship scheme became the bridge that connected Grenada with India, bringing forth a new chapter of hope and opportunity. The island needed strong hands and determined spirits to cultivate its land and contribute to its growth. The East Indians, with their courage and resilience, answered that call and helped overcome the challenges faced by the vacant sugar plantations. The indentureship scheme, born out of necessity, laid the foundation for the Indo-Grenadian community.

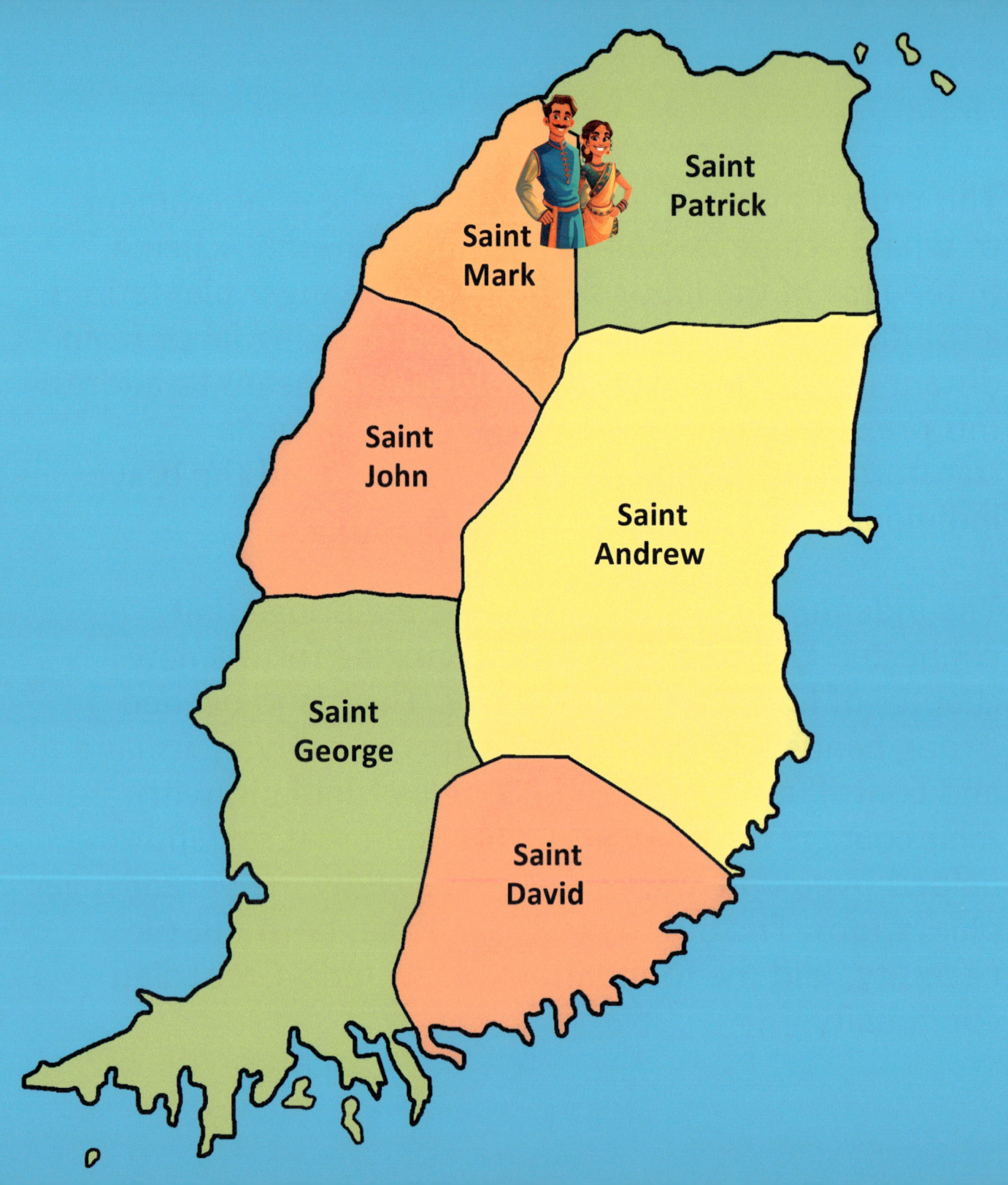

When the smaller ships entered Irwin's Bay, those onboard were taken to Belmont Estate in St. Patricks as a holding place. Today, Belmont Estate has grown to 400 acres, it has a restaurant and chocolate factory and even animals you can visit. There are even Indo-Grenadians whose ancestors came from India who still work and live close to there.

From there, they settled into Grenada and formed communities like those in the parishes of St. Marks and St. Patricks. Some East Indians went even further into other parts of Grenada as well. Although the indentureship scheme ended in 1885 with the arrival of the last ship, the contracts of some of those indentured labourers did not formally end until 1917. Some individuals chose to leave and go back to India while others stayed and formed these vibrant communities that still thrive today.

The plants in Grenada got a lot more colourful and the food even more flavorful when Indians came to the island. The reason for that is the spices, foods and flowers onboard the ships that brought East Indians to Grenada. These plants from India, include a lot the foods we enjoy today. For instance, Grenadas national dish is oil down which includes turmeric, an essential ingredient giving the dish its yellowish colour. Tumeric came from India.

Who likes mangoes? There are over 400 kinds of mango in Grenada and yes, they too came from India. Along with eggplant, jackfruit, moringa, christophene, govenour plum, damsel, cinnamon, sorrel, ginger, tamarind and clove, India has given us some yummy foods to eat.

Do you know how special clove was at one point? The clove trade was so lucrative, it was said cloves were four times more expensive than gold long ago and people preferred to be paid in cloves rather than other forms of payment!

Remember when East Indians first came to Grenada, they went onto many abandoned sugar plantations? Eventually, sugar was no longer bringing in the money it once had and cocoa and nutmeg became the foods mostly grown on these plantations. Grenada became the second largest producer of nutmeg in the world! It is such an important part of our culture and history that it became known as Black Gold and we became known as the Isle of Spice as a result. That explains why the nutmeg is on Grenada's national flag!

By the 1870s, many East Indians had invested in land, becoming integral members of Grenada and contributing to the cocoa and nutmeg industry. This contributed to the remarkable journey of East Indian laborers evolving into proud landowners, cultivating cocoa, provisions, and livestock. The industrious spirit of these individuals showcased their dedication to transforming Grenada's agricultural landscape. East Indians illustrated their determination to not only secure their place in Grenadian society but also to contribute significantly to the island's economic development. To this day, you still have individuals of East Indian descent working with cocoa to make outstanding chocolate!

Two visionaries of cocoa production were Norbert Nyack and LL Ramdhanny, prominent landowners and cocoa producers who played pivotal roles in Grenada's economic growth. This began the emergence of Grenada as a key player in the global cocoa market, thanks to the foresight and innovation of these remarkable individuals.

The descendants of East Indian immigrants not only became landowners and began making a difference in agriculture, but they also paved the way for future generations in agriculture, law, medicine, education, and more. Their families grew and made contributions to various fields. For instance, Mac Donald College was founded by the Grenada East Indian Cultural Association in 1963 and it currently houses the bust of Mahatma Gandhi, one of India's most important leaders. This college is a mainstay in Grenada's tertiary education and has produced many graduates since its inception.

Jennifer Japal-Issac is also an important person to mention as she is one of the first female Indo-Grenadian doctors. She is still practicing and making pioneering contributions to healthcare today. We celebrate the commitment of the Indo-Grenadian community to education and the profound impact it has had on shaping Grenada's intellectual landscape.

Other family names of East Indian descent present in Grenada's history include Budhlall, Nyack, Bhola, Ramdhanny, Japal, Budhoo, DeGale, DeAllie, Narayan, and Noel.

As time went on, one demonstration of Indo-Grenadians embracing their mixed heritage and being influenced by intermarriage and cultural exchanges was the adoption of Western names for Indian ones. This in part was due to the role of Christianity in shaping Indo-Grenadian identities. They have embraced a blended cultural heritage while preserving the essence of their roots. These shifting identities provides a deeper understanding of the cultural mosaic that defines contemporary Indo-Grenadian communities.

One of the biggest and most delightful displays and traces of East Indian culture can be seen in Grenada's food, music, and dance. Although cultural practices evolved, traces of Indian culture persist in Grenada in these ways. Think about the aromas of traditional Indian spices and curry, the rhythms of Grenadian-Indian music, the joyful movements of dance to the yummy flavors wrapped up as a roti and the comforting warmth of dhal over rice, to the rhythmic beats of traditional Indian tunes, the essence of Indo-Grenadian cultural preservation has survived generations. Despite the evolution of cultural practices, certain elements have become integral to the fabric of Grenada's identity.

Honouring the vestiges of East Indian culture in Indo-Grenadian and Grenadian lives is alive and well. Embracing this heritage and exchanging cultural knowledge is something to be celebrated and is sparking a renewed interest in Grenadian history. It also serves as a point of pride to know the depths and intricacies of our culture and history, a colorful past that influences our future.

Celebrate with us, the resilience of Indo-Grenadians and their commitment to preserving and revitalizing their cultural heritage and its influences on Grenada's cultural landscape. Today, Grenada proudly showcases its diverse population, where different cultures and communities thrive together. Reflect on this journey through history, celebrating the enduring legacy of Indo-Grenadians in shaping Grenada's vibrant and diverse culture.

Made in the USA
Columbia, SC
13 November 2024